Coloring Book For Adults
Animals and Patterns
Relaxation

101 Images Beginner to Advanced

www.vibrant-puzzle-books.com
Join us @
Facebook: VibrantBooks
Twitter: BooksVibrant
Pinterest: Vibrant_Books
Instagram:
adult_coloring_puzzle_books

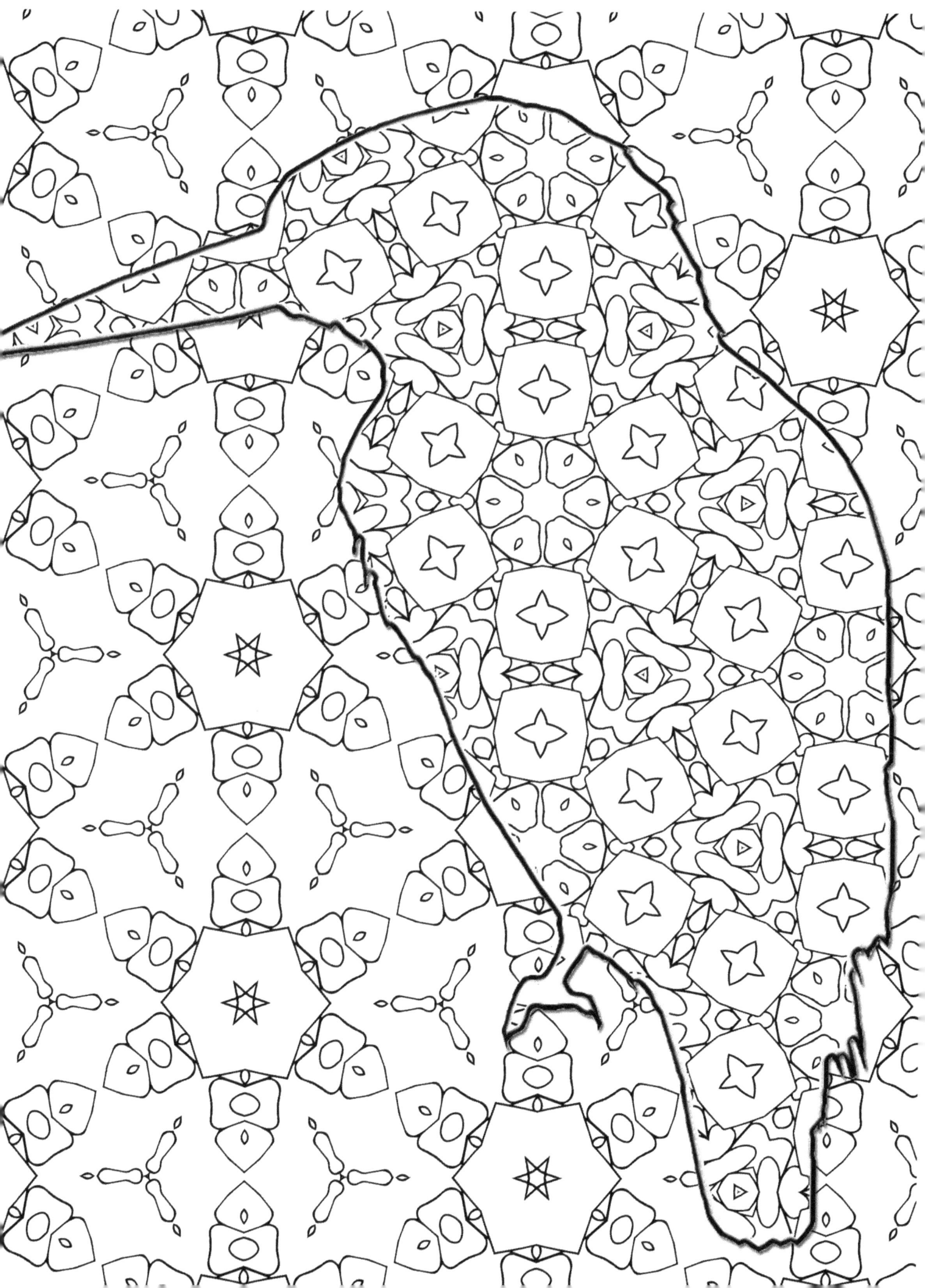

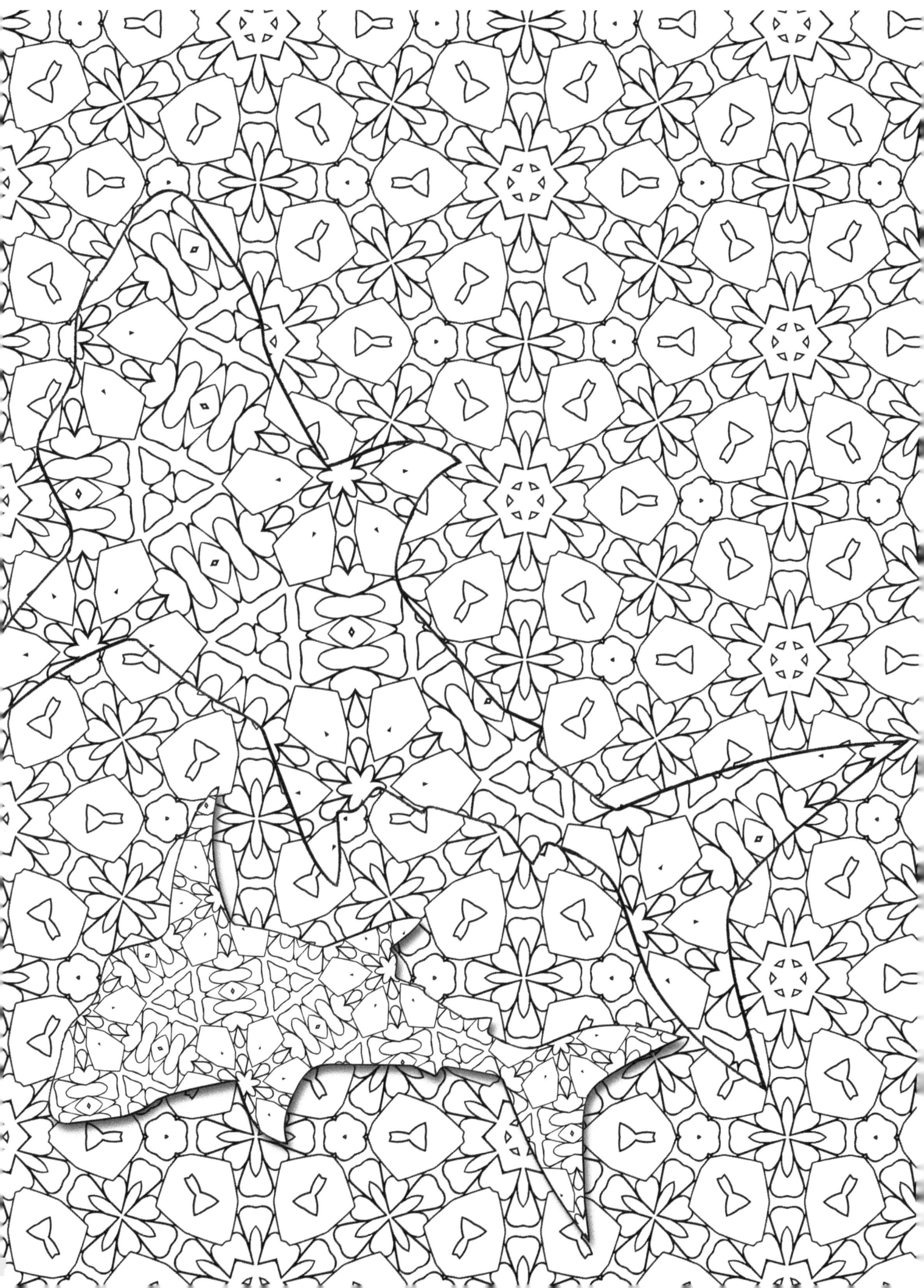

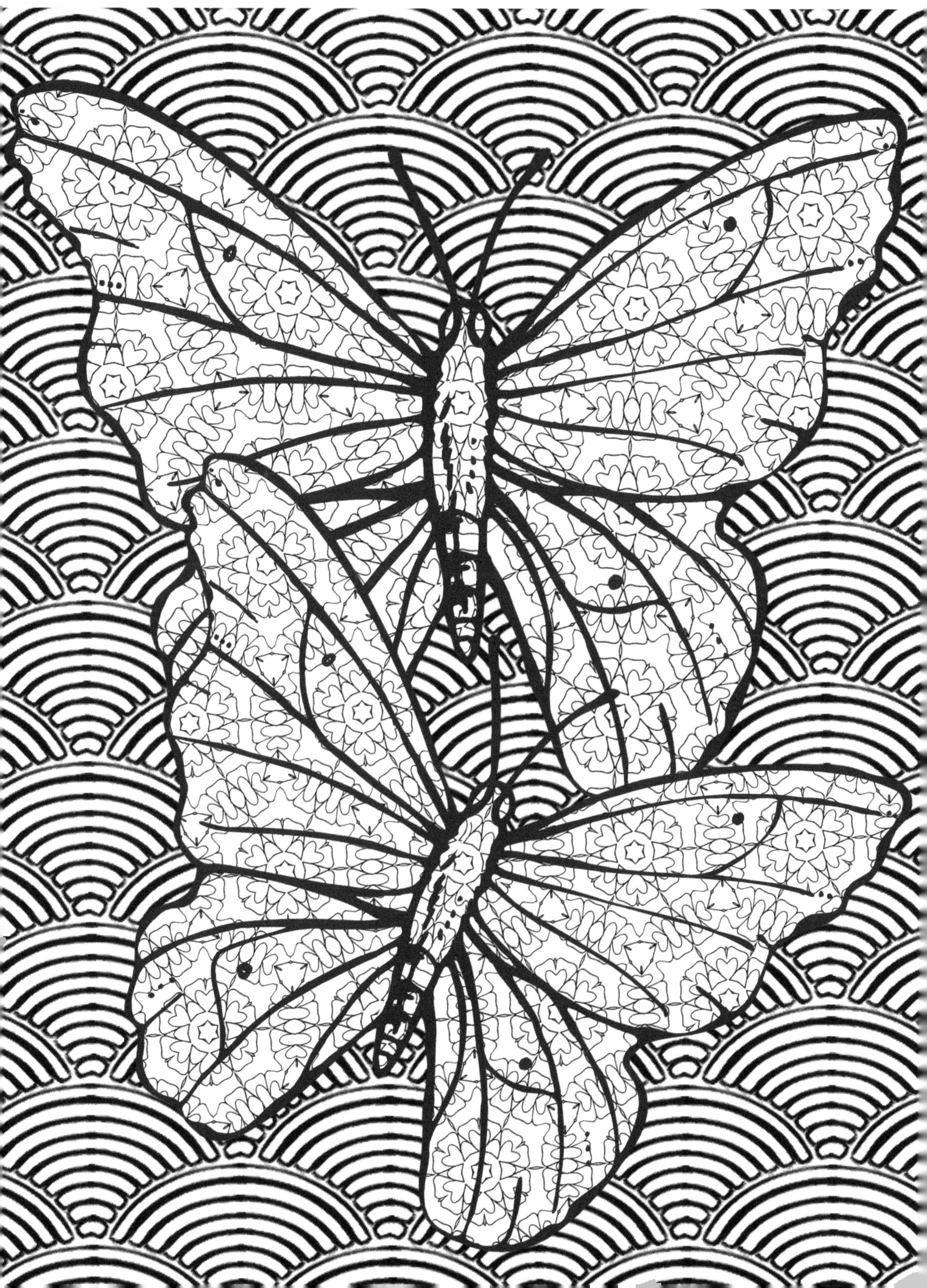

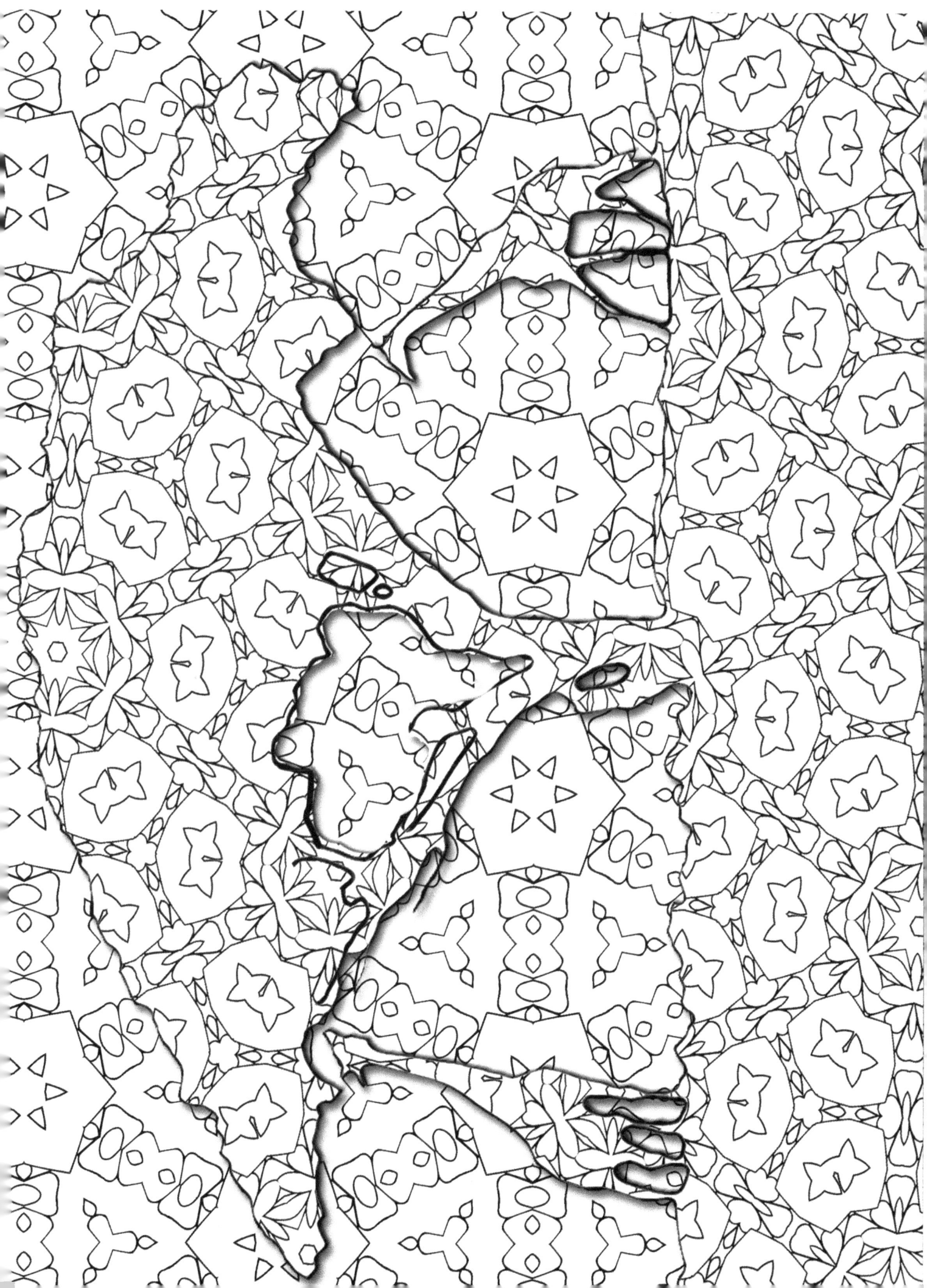

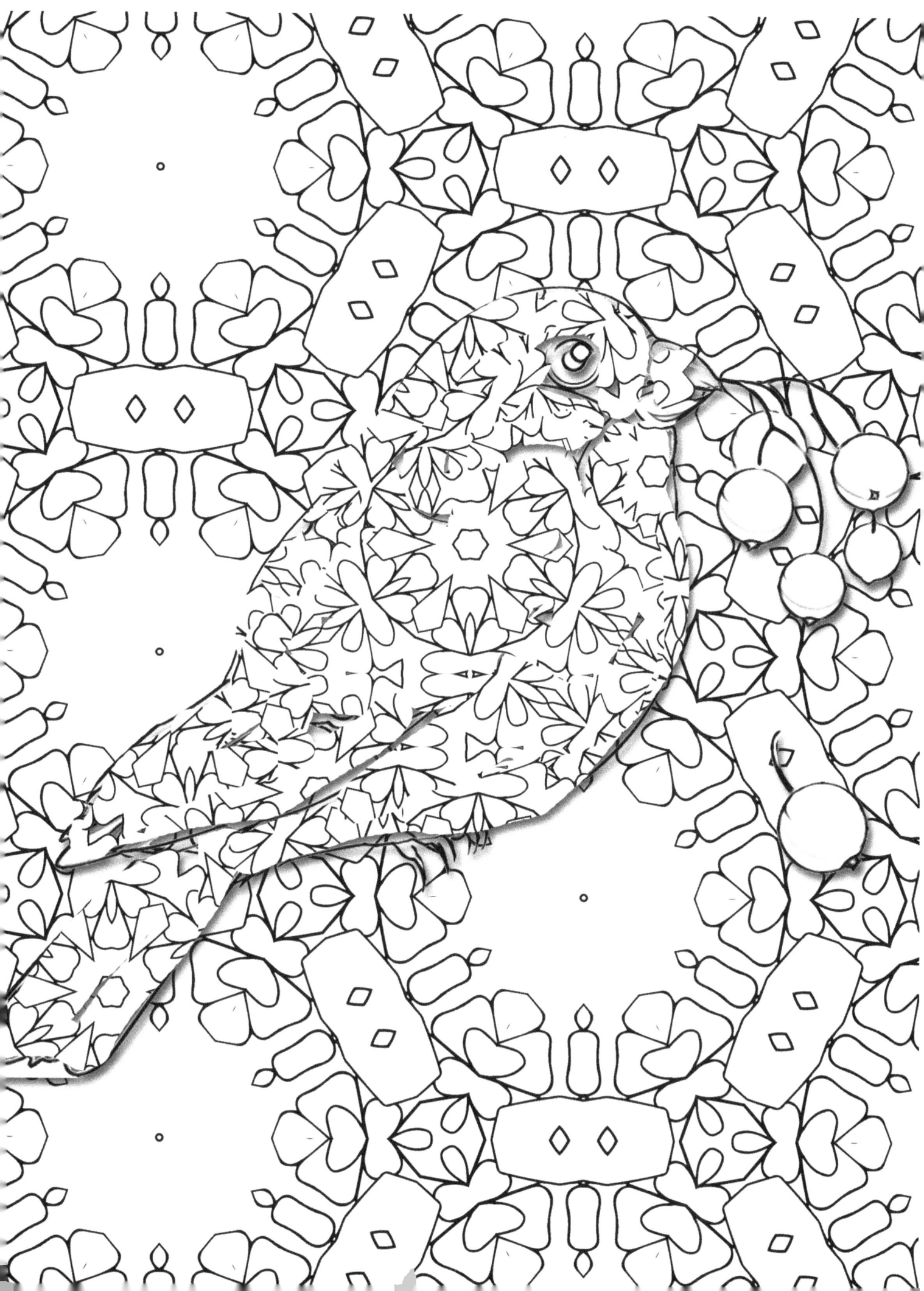

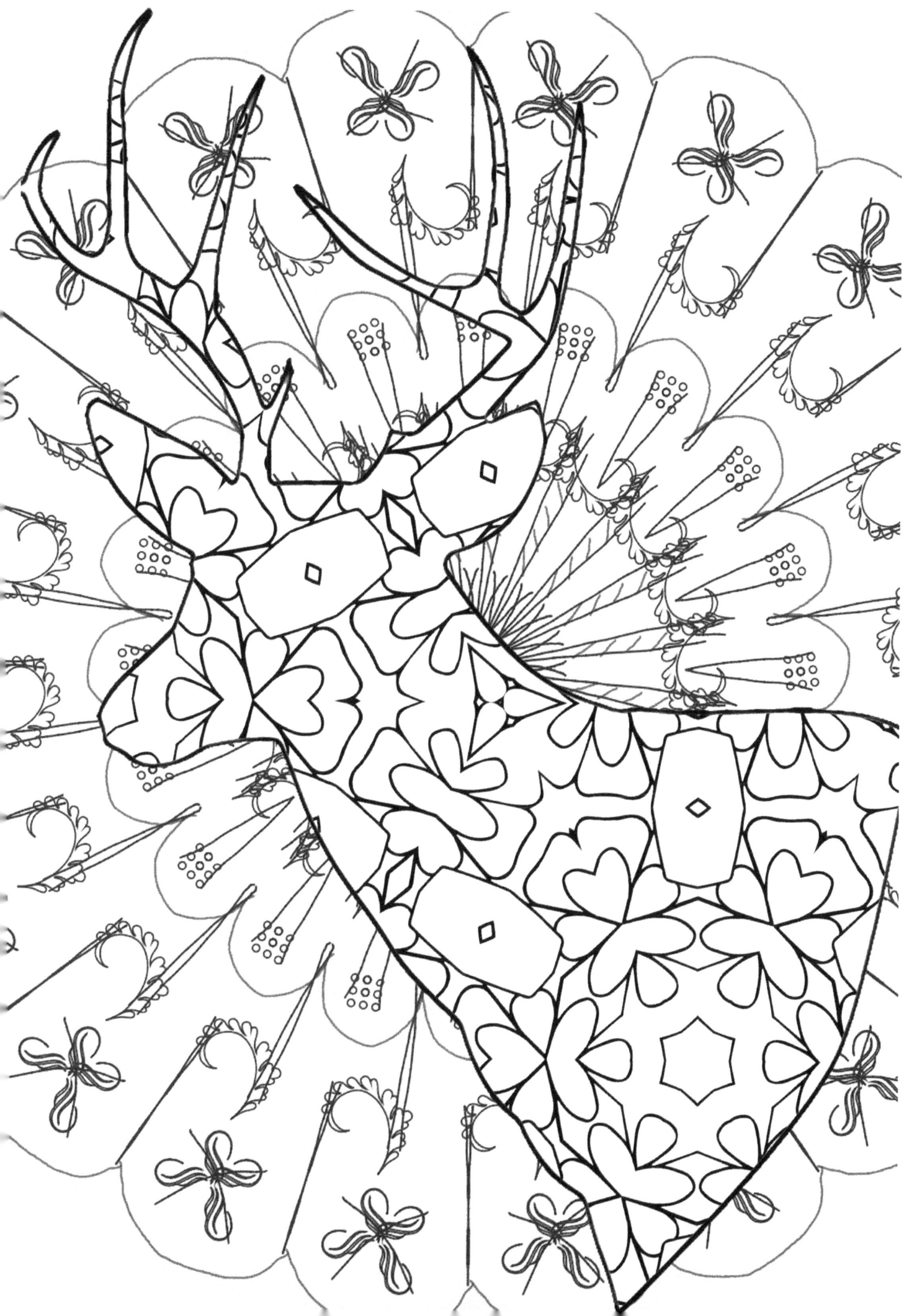

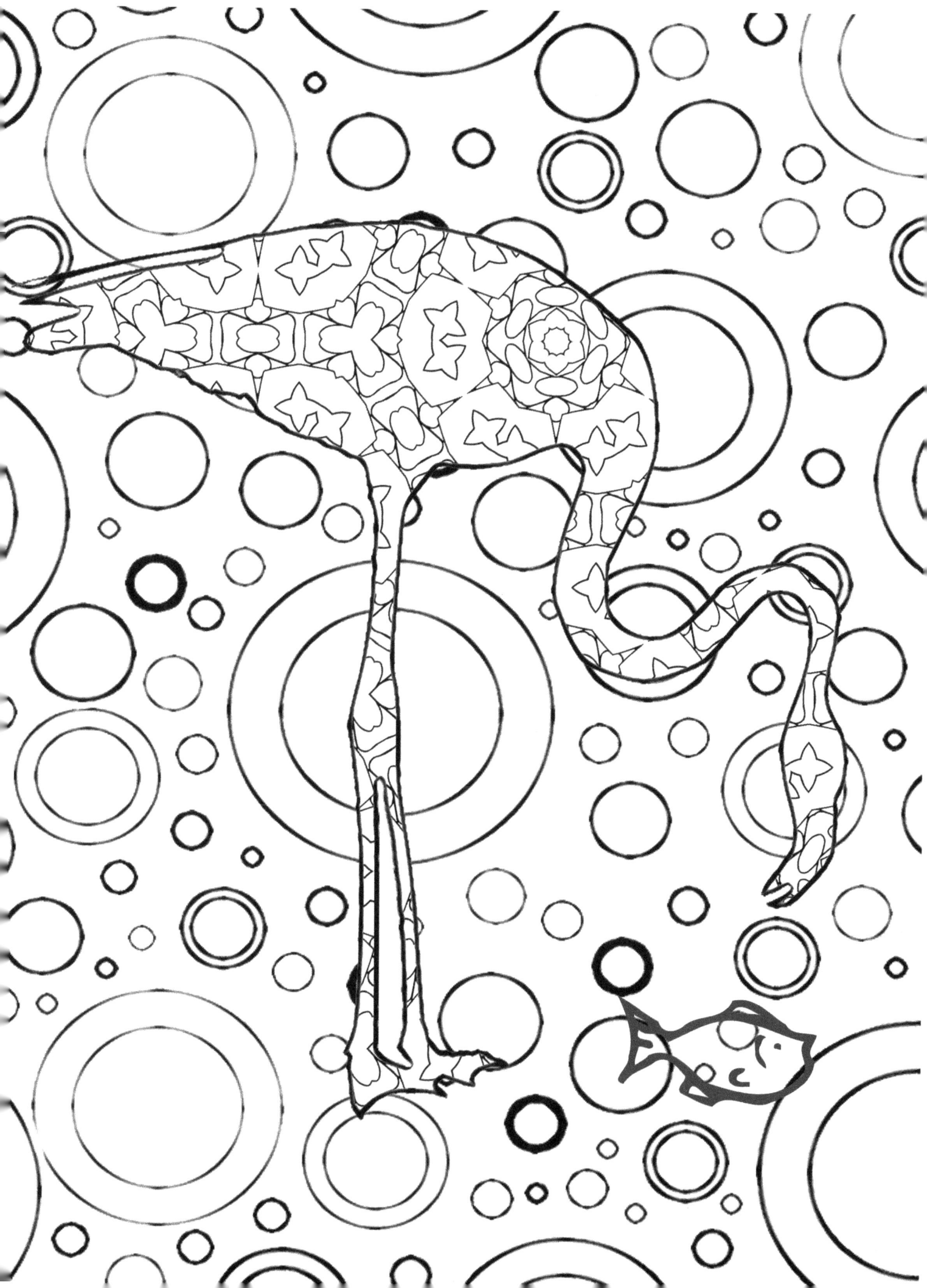

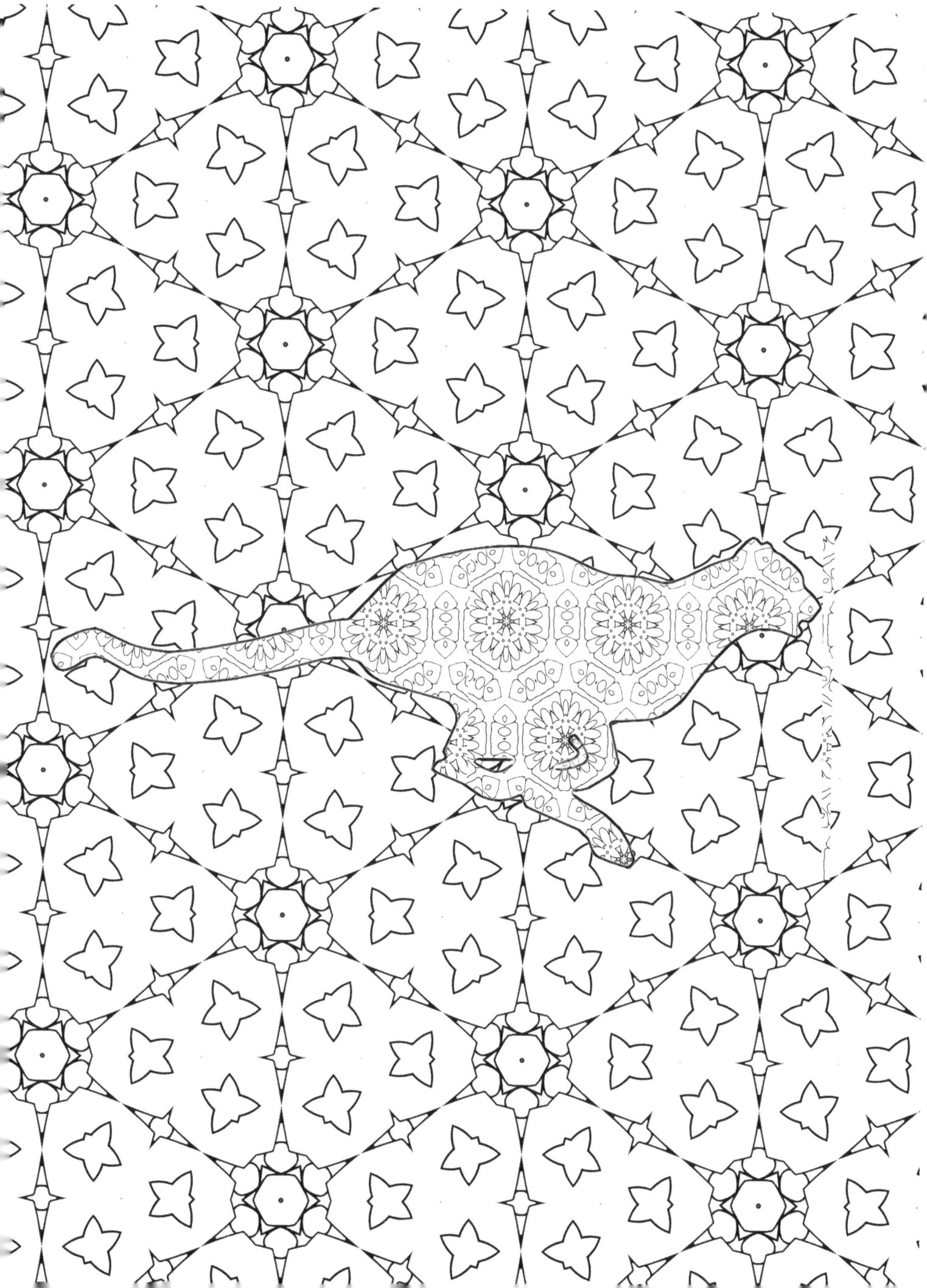

Also By Vibrant Books:

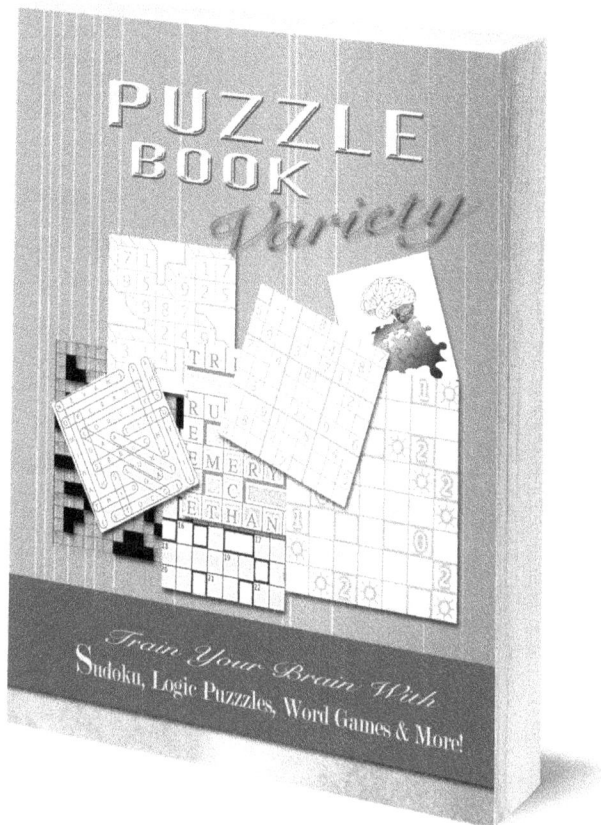

200 PUZZLES

Train your Brain With Sudoku, Logic Puzzles, Word Games & More! Level: Medium to Medium Hard

Available at most bookstores on and offline. And on our website at www.

www.vibrant-puzzle-books.com
Join us @
 Facebook: VibrantBooks
Twitter: BooksVibrant
Pinterest: Vibrant_Books
Instagram: adult_coloring_puzzle_books

www.ingramcontent.com/pod-product-compliance
Lightning Source LLC
Chambersburg PA
CBHW080621030426
42336CB00018B/3042